THE TOP HAT

Popular costume from the Gard region of France, early 1800s.
Author's collection.

THE TOP HAT

AN

ILLUSTRATED

HISTORY OF

ITS STYLING AND

MANUFACTURE

BY

DEBBIE

HENDERSON, PH.D.

The Wild Goose Press
Yellow Springs, Ohio

Published by The Wild Goose Press, 504 Phillips Street, Yellow Springs, OH 45387
Produced in conjunction with the National Hat Museum, Durham, North Carolina.

Photographs

We are grateful to the following for permission to reproduce the photographs that appear on these pages: Bath Museum of Costume, p. 36; John Brandwood, back cover; Cincinnati Art Museum, pp. 11, 23, 31; Cincinnati Historical Society, p. 8; George Eastman House, pp. 20, 48; Hat Life Publications, pp. 58, 60, 61, 65, 66, 68, 70; Ken Jewell, p. 52; Ohio Historical Society, p. 49; Roswell Art Museum, p. 45; Stockport Heritage Museum, pp. 18, 28, 40, 45, 47, 55, back cover.

Book design by Jane Baker

ISBN 0-9651153-3-X

Library of Congress Card Number: 00-105598

Without the photographic assistance and browsing persistence of my husband, Jon Barlow Hudson, neither the hat collection nor the continuing discovery of hat history would have been possible. Nor would any of this information have reached the reader without the encouragement and book design of Jane Baker. To these two this book is dedicated.

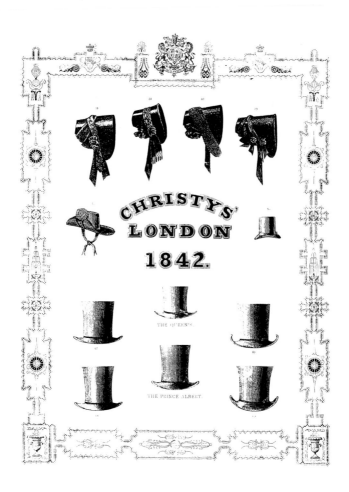

"When you meet people, you look them in the face and your first, most immediate impressions about them are received from the head and from anything that your acquaintance, new or old, may have chosen, or needed, to put upon it."
Ann Saunders, F.S.A.
Fellow, University College, London, England

Contents

Unknown gentleman wearing fur felt top hat, c. 1850.
Courtesy Cincinnati Historical Society.

Illustrations

In Central Africa, the conqueror and man of great parts is distinguished for his preeminence by the wearing of a high hat, very much resembling the stovepipe hat of civilized lands, but the brim is on top. There is certainly something indescribable but elevating in the high hat, and it naturally receives the greatest attention from both the wearer and producer.—E. G. Glave, St. Nicholas, *reprinted in* The Sartorial Art Journal, *August 1890*

Figure 1. Black silk plush top hat, crown 7, brim 1⁵/₈.
Cincinnati Art Museum.

Figure 2. Richard Mansfield as "Beau Brummell,"
Madison Square Theater, June 16, 1890. Author's collection.

THE
TOP
HAT

A man's hat is his crowning glory; the top hat made him king. But what is the point of wearing a four- to ten-inch tube on the top of your head? For that is what the top hat appears to be: a tube. It is nicknamed a stove pipe, a chimney pot, or a bell topper. This accessory may be an oddity to us today, yet for centuries men and women have worn them, even to the point of causing alarm. In January 1797 John Heathcote caused a riot by wearing a "tall structure having a shiny luster and calculated to frighten people."[1] Freudian psychologist J. C. Flugel believed that protuberant cylinders, like top hats and cigars, were phallic symbols.[2] Clothing historian Colin McDowell states that the "high, hard hat represented the power of political conservatism and the rule of the status quo"[3] (see Figure 2).

Perhaps the most familiar images of the top hat are of Abraham Lincoln in his stovepipe or Fred Astaire in his elegant, glossy opera hat—both simple, black, tall, and only slightly curved. These were the typical toppers with no extreme shaping, coloring, or styling; these were the norm. The norm is what we generally picture when we think "top hat," but actually a wide variety of top hats were manufactured and worn. The 1899 Christy Hat Company Catalogue pictures over 400 hat styles, including toppers, bowlers, straws, and caps. More than half the choices are top hats. This variety of shapes and styles, materials and colors (all within the sartorial boundaries of acceptable fashion) allowed the wearer to create his own unique character—his metaphorical male crown.

Figure 3. Showman Ted Lewis waving his topper.
Author's collection.

HISTORY

Hats for Fall and Winter, August, 1891

"The indications are that in silks the shape will be a pronounced bell, with a wider and gracefully rolled brim. In some instance, indeed, it will probably be carried to an extreme, and thus becoming a caricature, the bell shape, like any fashion that is overdone, will rapidly subside. At the same time the graceful hat of two seasons ago, with its moderately tapering crown, will be selected by many of our best dressers as being the most sensible shape shown in many seasons. As for bands, the overshot silks of two inches in width, which made their appearance abroad about a year ago, are coming to this side, and it may be that they will supplant the cloth bands, from which fashion would welcome a change."—The Sartorial Art Journal

"Between correct morning attire and either afternoon or evening dress, there is as marked a difference as there is between a silk hat and a derby."—The Sartorial Art Journal, November 1897

Figure 4. Tall hats were worn for centuries. James Douglas, Earl of Morton, Regent of Scotland, wearing a late-16th- or early-17th-century version constructed of fur felt. Author's collection.

The possible ancestor of the top hat, the Sugar Loaf or Steeple hat, was made of fur felt; it could be left plain or decorated with ribbons and feathers to indicate the status or group affiliation of its wearer. Clothing historian Madeleine Ginsburg writes, "The fashionable shape for hats changed slowly but definitely during the first half of the 17th century. The Thirty Years' War (1618–48) brought military styles into everyone's experience. High crowns were fashionable at the beginning of the period, with high pointed tops, dubbed Sugar Loaves or Steeples. They began to disappear as they were too difficult to keep on."[4] This style hat was worn by both ladies and gentlemen in the seventeenth century. The size of the

Figure 5. The broad-brimmed and high-crowned hat of the 17th century was constructed from two pieces of felt. Author's collection.

crown and the wide brim required that the hat be made from two separate pieces of felt, sewn together where the crown met the brim. The stitching was hidden by a cord or decoration. The Victoria and Albert Museum in London has two hats dating from the early 1600s with this construction. When brims became somewhat narrower, the entire hat could be shaped from a single cone of fur felt.

In 1585 Philip Stubbs wrote about fashionable hats:

Sometimes they use them sharp on the crown, peaking up like the spear or shaft of a steeple, standing a quarter of a yard above the crown of their heads, some more, some less, as please the fancies of their inconstant minds. Some others are flat and broad on the crown like the battlements of a house. Another sort have round crowns, sometimes with one kind of band, sometimes with another, now black, now white, now russet, now red, now green, now yellow, now this, now that, never content with one colour or fashion two days to an end. And thus in vanity they spend the Lord's treasure, consuming their golden years and silver days in wickedness and sin.

And as the fashions be rare and strange, so is the stuff whereof their hats be made divers also; for some are of silk, some of velvet, some of taffetie, some of sarcenet, some of wool; and, which is more curious, some of a certain kind of fine hair. These they call Beaver Hats, of twenty, thirty, or forty shillings price fetched from beyond the seas, from whence a great sort of other vanities do come beside.

—"A Day at a Hat Factory," *The Penny Magazine,* January 1841

Keeping the top hat in place was indeed tricky, because in the beginning hats were blocked in a round shape, although human heads are variously dented ovals. One solution for a tighter fit was to sew into the sweat band a string that could be drawn in to help secure the hat to the head. The second and more suitable solution was to make the hat in an oval shape. By the nineteenth century this was customary. A wealthy gentleman could take this reformulation a step further: he had his head shape accurately measured and these measurements kept on file by his hatter; whenever he ordered a new hat it could be shaped exactly to the pattern of his uniquely formed skull.

A mechanical device called a conformateur (see Figure 58) was used to record the exact shape of the head. More recent devices, such as a bendable metal ring, are now used along with still functioning or rebuilt conformateurs. When gentlemen have their hats custom made, the conformateur duplicates the wearer's head shape so accurately that the hat fits like a glove. The hat so perfectly matches his head, that even a strong wind cannot blow it off.

Not only was the top hat popular among the gentry, but an austerely plain version was adopted by religious sects, such as the Quakers and the Puritans. Even today members of other religious groups, including Shakers, Brethren, Mennonites, and Hassidic Jews, wear the black, lower-crowned, flat, wide-brimmed hat. The current hat manufacturers, Hatco (Stetson, Resistol, and Dobbs), Langenberg, and Bollman, attribute a large segment of their business to religious groups. Costume critic Colin McDowell explains their consistent use of this style: " religious sects are reluctant to allow variation in their members' dress because the strength of the movement frequently rests on the denial of individuality and the subjugation of personal choice."[5] Figure 6 shows a typical Quaker style hat (crown height 5 inches and brim width 3¾ inches). This particular hat, a 1908 replica of the style worn in the

Figure 6. "The Quaker" reproduction hat made of silk plush. Stockport Heritage Museum.

eighteenth century, is even labeled "The Quaker" by its manufacturer, Tess and Company. In the seventeenth and eighteenth centuries hats were made from fur or wool felt, as were the nineteenth-century fashionable top hats. Most top hat construction changed to silk plush when beaver fur became too expensive, and men's dressing guides accepted the silken sheen of the new top hat. Today, silk plush top hats are no longer made, requiring top hats once again to be constructed from fur or wool felt.

Figure 7. The Quaker Lace Company used the image of a Quaker on its boxes. Author's collection.

A lapse in the wearing of tall hats occurred when wigs became the fashionable head adornment of gentlemen in the eighteenth century. Adoption of the tricorn and bicorn fit with the times. They represented a new look for new ideologies: an easily flattened head piece that could be carried or held under the arm and not obstruct the styled wig that was in vogue (see Figure 9). The top hat's absence was short-lived, for while the previously mentioned religious groups remained faithful to their styles, in the 1790s the narrow cylinder, however uncomfortable, reappeared on the heads of fashionable gentlemen (Figure 10). By the nineteenth century it had become the irrepressible symbol of prestige and authority. Fashion magazines included the top hat as desirable attire, and fashion plates pictured it as essential for formal wear (see Figure 11).

Figure 8. Calling card illustrated by a fur felt top hat, c. 1870. Courtesy George Eastman House.

*Figure 9. The popular 18th-century tricorn worn by
Richard Watson, Bishop of Landaff. Author's collection.*

*Figure 10. The style of top hat worn in the late 18th century.
Author's collection.*

Figure 11. Three gentlemen wearing three variations of a tall hat. Le Follet, 1822. Author's collection.

In her 1858 guide to men's fashion Margaret C. Conkling wrote, "But while care is taken to avoid the display of undue attention to adornment of the outer man, everything approaching to indifference or neglect, in that regard, should be considered equally reprehensible. I unhesitatingly counsel you to dress in the fashion and the prevailing mode; an entirely fresh-looking fashionable black hat and carefully-fitted modish boots, white gloves, and a soft, thin, white handkerchief."[6]

By the nineteenth century, the top hat was, like skirts today, worn in many lengths, colors, textures, and materials—from the most expensive beaver fur to imported Tuscan straw (see Figures 12–14). When beaver fur

Figure 12. Fur felt top hat. Author's collection.

Figure 13. Pearl gray silk plush top hat. Crown 4³/₄, brim 1³/₄.
Cincinnati Art Museum.

Figure 14. Straw top hat. Crown 5¹/₂, brim 2¹/₄.
Cincinnati Art Museum.

became scarce, hats were made of a silk plush fabric covering a lacquered calico or cardboard shell. Some even folded, both vertically and horizontally, so as to fit snugly under the arm or under an opera seat. On formal occasions, well-dressed gentlemen were incomplete without their top hats (Figure 15). Other classes aped the gentry:

Figure 15. Fashion illustration from Jno. J. Mitchell Co. Catalogue, May 1901.

coachmen (Figure 16) wore both silk and felt toppers, dandies copied the fashionable by wearing more severely shaped and tilted versions (Figure 17), and both men and women adopted the top hat as essential equestrian gear (Figures 18 and 19). Even the police wore leather top hats in the early 1800s. The one in the Stockport Museum collection is made of leather, bound in brass with the Stockport Coat of Arms painted on the front (Figure 20).

Figure 16. Fashion illustration from Jno. J. Mitchell Co. Catalogue, January 1900.

Fashion plates pictured the current mode—the exact dimension of the crown, the degree of curve to the brim (Figure 21). Illustrations and portrait photographs that followed the invention of the daguerreotype in the 1840s indicate that the height of the hat, the tapering of the crown, and the curl of the brim vary throughout the century (Figures 22 and 23). From 1790 to the 1830s, the gentleman's top hat was a slender six- to seven-inch crown with an extremely narrow brim curving downward in both front and back. During the 1840s and '50s, the brims broadened to almost three inches and the crown tapered severely into what some people might call the "Mad Hatter" style, a name derived from that character in *Alice in Wonderland* (Figures 24 and 25).

Lewis Carroll's reference to the "madness" attributed to hat makers is based on fact. In the initial stage of making the fur cone, mercuric nitrate was used to roughen the

Figure 17. A dandy in his felt top hat.

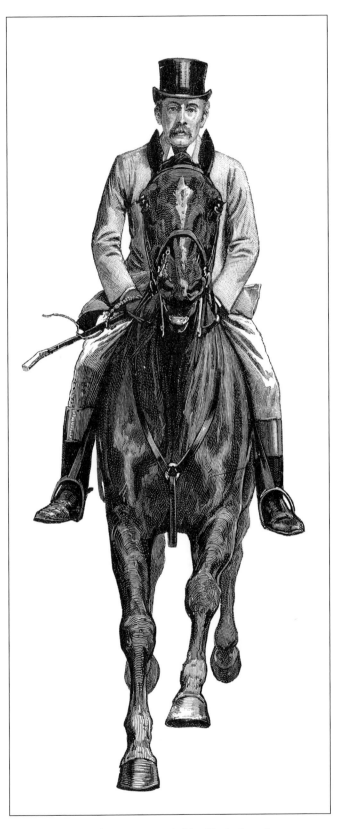

Figure 18. A sportsman in his silk plush top hat.

Figure 19. The famous European actress Disderi, wearing her top hat for riding. Author's collection.

*Figure 20. Policeman's leather top hat.
Stockport Heritage Museum.*

Opposite Page:
Top—Figure 21. Fashion illustration from The Sartor, *London, 1871.*
*Bottom—Figure 22. Gentleman wearing a silk plush top hat
(and enjoying his image).*

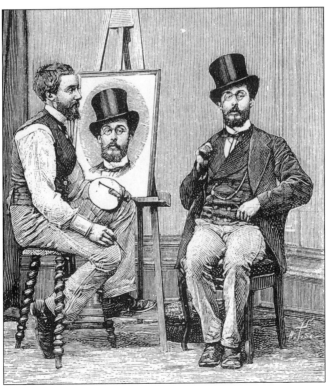

1790s

1820s

1860s

1870s

1900

Figure 23. The general shapes of top hats from the 18th to the 20th centuries. Drawings by Emily Schmidt.

Opposite Page:
Top—Figure 24. "Mad Hatter" style top hat, dated 1844.
Crown 8 inches, brim 3 inches. Cincinnati Art Museum.
Bottom—Figure 25. Unknown gentleman wearing a top hat in the
"Mad Hatter" style. Author's collection.

hairs, thereby helping the fibers lock together to form a tighter bond and producing felt of a better quality. This process, which turned the fur orange, was called carrotting. When the hat body was ironed into its finished shape, mercury was released as vapor. Breathing the fumes caused the hatters to develop what were called "hatter's shakes"—mercury poisoning, which led to what appeared to be madness. Later experiments showed that this condition could be alleviated with better ventilation. Today, substitute chemicals that cause no adverse effects are used.

The foibles of fashion are puzzling. The 1850s fashion preferred the eight-inch crown with straighter sides (the stovepipe) to the lower and more curved line of the 1860s. Lincoln's inaugural hat of 1860 was not the iconic stovepipe of his campaign days in the 1850s, but a lower, slightly curved, silk plush—not a beaver felt—hat. Crowns

Figure 26. Child's medium-height crown hat of silk plush. Crown 3¹/4, brim 1¹/2. Author's collection

Figure 27. Low-crown black silk plush hat. Crown 4⁷/8, brim 2³/8. Author's collection.

*Figure 28. Tintype of unknown gentleman wearing a
medium-crown hat. Author's collection.*

became taller again in the 1870s and lower once more in
the 1890s.

Until it was replaced by the bowler and then the fe-
dora in the twentieth century, the lower version of the top
hat (Figures 26–29) was popular with the working man
during the nineteenth century:

> The Wellington, a top hat designed by the Iron Duke, had
> a reverse tapered flat crown and a curled brim. A shortened ver-
> sion was popular with the artisan class, symbolized by the char-
> acter of Mr. Pickwick of Dickensian tales. —"The Atherstone
> Hatters," Wilson & Stafford Limited, 1998

In a photograph of Abraham Lincoln's second Inaugural
Address taken in front of the Capitol in 1864, most of the
men listening to Lincoln's speech are wearing the low top
hat, while the men surrounding Lincoln are wearing the
taller, seven-inch version.[7] Very few of these shorter hats

Figure 29. Unknown gentleman holding a medium-crown straw hat. Author's collection.

are found in museums and private collections, since few have been saved, possibly because they belonged to men who wore them out and discarded them. Collections tend to contain donations of formal top hats that were worn less frequently and were more carefully stored by the more prominent citizenry.

This shorter-crowned hat might easily have been forgotten due to the choice of the larger hat for movie heroes. The big hat was king until Clint Eastwood made the low-crowned, broad-brimmed hat, similar to the Mexican charreria hat or the Spanish flat-brimmed hat, his signature model in most of his Western films. The mail order catalogue for Dirty Billy's Hats, specializing in historic reproductions, calls this style the "Pale Rider," the name of the film Eastwood made in 1985 wearing just such a hat.

Figure 30. Unknown man and children with their varied hat styles. Author's collection.

The twentieth century and the adoption of automobile travel have been less kind to the topper, an accessory of inconvenient size. Adaptations were made, as exemplified by gentlemen having to wear a top hat to the opera: since there soon became too little room in the coat check for all the top hats, the folding opera hat was invented. This was made possible by a Frenchman, Antoine Gibus, who perfected a folding spring already invented in 1820, which allowed the silk covering to collapse like an accordion into a thin dinner-plate size that slipped neatly into wire brackets under the theatre seats. Gibus filed his patents between 1834 and 1840. Opera hats are still manufactured in a "beautifully finished silk satin" and described as adding "elegance and distinction for that very formal evening."[8]

Collapsing a hat into a convenient package was not new. The bicorn of a century before could be folded flat, so as to easily be held or tucked under the arm. Another top hat folded from side to side (Figures 31–33). It reminds one of a truncated bicorn, but is round and tall

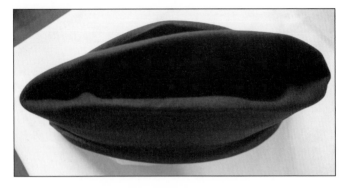

*Figure 31. Circumfolding dress hat, top view.
Bath Museum of Costume.*

Figure 32. Circumfolding dress hat, side view.

Figure 33. Circumfolding dress hat, interior view.

when on the wearer's head. It is made of fur felt and lined with red silk. Looking at the hat, one is aware of the folded felt that allows for the expansion of the shape over the ear. A continuous, unseamed piece of felt forms both crown and brim. On the wearer's head, the hat appears as a stiffened cylinder, but because the frame is felt and not cardboard, as in the silk plush, it can be folded. C. Willett and Phillis Cunnington in *The Handbook of English Costume in the 19th Century* called this style a "circumfolding dress hat" whose "crowns are made to fold in the middle so as to be carried under the arm."[9]

At least four of these hats exist, two at the Costume Institute in Bath, England, one at the Victoria and Albert Museum in London, and one in the Snowshill Costume Collection, Berrington Hall, Herefordshire. One of the two folding hats in the Bath Museum is in remarkably good condition. The felt retains its tight, smooth consistency, indicating a high beaver fur content. The vibrant red silk lining extends slightly beyond what would be considered normal in a blocked, brimmed hat, continuing onto the underside of the brim. When the hat is expanded to fit over the head, the side brims fold down a bit to obscure the lining. Few extant hats and even fewer fashion illustrations suggest that not many of these hats were produced and that the wearing of them was short-lived. Fortunately, in an illustration from *Lady's Magazine,* 1835, gentlemen are pictured with these hats (Figure 34). The gentleman on the left holds his behind his back while the gentleman on the right has his hat next to him on the sofa. Another fashion-plate in *The Gentleman's Magazine* of May 1829 also pictures the hat in the hand of a gentleman dressed in evening wear.

The stylishly curled top hat shape has come full circle from the flat-folding, under-arm accessory to the smartly flanged doorman's uniform. But what has become of it since hats ceased to be the key to a gentleman's outfit? The top hat has refused to die. The stiff vertical has softened to a floppy parody of itself, perhaps via *The Cat in the Hat* by Dr. Seuss (Figure 35). (What would Freudians make of this?) Younger members of society find it appealing, colorful, and perhaps more akin to clown costuming

Figure 34. Two gentlemen, one with top hat behind his back, the other with his lying to his side. "Le Follet Courier des Salons," Lady's Magazine, c. 1835

Figure 35. Glen Evan wearing the latest in soft fabric top hats.

than to its original sign of elegance and status. The shape is an allusion to past glory, but like all clothing in this multicultural world, self-parody encourages humor over serious decorum, the debasement of status, the gentleman as clown. Whatever the connotations of the present top hat, it can still be seen at weddings, funerals, and definitely at the races, atop Uncle Sam, and still crowning society's elite.

Figure 36. Uncle Sam wearing a fur felt top hat.
Author's collection.

The Museum of Hatting - Stockport

Come and see the UK's only museum dedicated to the hatting industry!

- Working Machinery
- William White's Shop
- William Plant's Hat Block Workshop
- Audio Visual Room
- Mad Hatter's Tea Room

OPEN EVERY SUNDAY

 Stockport Metropolitan Borough Council

Figure 37. Brochure from the Museum of Hatting at Stockport.

MANUFACTURE

"How is a beaver hat made? It is not improbable that we should receive a dozen different answers. One would think it is cast in a mould; another, that the beaver's fur is in some way woven into a kind of cloth, and put on a stiff foundation; but perhaps not one would have an idea of the beautiful process of felting, *which is the groundwork of the whole theory of hat-making. A beaver hat consists mainly of two parts,—the* body *and the* covering; *the former of which is made of fine wool and coarse fur, mixed, felted, stiffened, and shaped; and the latter of beaver fur, made to adhere to the body by the process of felting. Wool and fur constitute therefore the main ingredients employed. For hats of inferior quality, coarse wool is employed for the body, and coarser fur, or sometimes fine wool, for the covering."—"A Day at a Hat-Factory,"* The Penny Magazine, *January 1841*

Top hats originally were made of fur or wool felt. Beaver made the strongest felt and could be mixed with hare, rabbit, nutria, or any number of furs. Another technique, which created an elegant looking hat but cost far less, was felting the more expensive beaver fur onto the surface of a rabbit fur or wool felt hat body. An even less expensive hat material was wool felt, which could be shaped or blocked into any of the fur felt hat styles. Even though wool felt is less durable, it was and remains today the mainstay of less expensive hats. Hat catalogues offered the customer choices not only in style but in price. The 1889 Taylor Bros. & Co. catalogue offers fur felt hats in the two- to three-dollar range (wholesale), while comparable styles in wool range from fifty cents to a dollar (see Figures 38 and 39). Western hats follow the same price differentiation in catalogues such as Stockman-Farmer, Stetson, Denver Dry Goods, Anderson Bros., and N. Porter. The same price difference is found in hat stores today.

To produce the thousands of hats needed each year, hundreds of thousands of animal pelts were required by hat makers. The Hudson Bay Company, the North East

BROADWAY

Spring · Style · of · Silk · Hat

· · 1889 · ·

Quantity.	Price.
......Dozen No. 130, Men's Silk Hats, No. 4.....................	$42.00
......Dozen No. 131, Men's Silk Hats, No. 3.............	48.00
......Dozen No. 132, Men's Silk Hats, No. 2.................... ...	54.00
......Dozen No. 133, Men's Silk Hats, No. 1.....................	60.00

Never let an Account run past due, and under no circumstances allow one to be placed in the hands of an attorney for collection. Good, reliable, honorable wholesale firms invariably refuse to sell a merchant when this occurs—if they know it. There are Jobbers who continue to sell storekeepers when they know the storekeepers have been sued. These same Jobbers are unscrupulous, have no conscience, and make a storekeeper pay an enormous profit because they know his credit is poor.

Figure 38. Page from the 1889 Taylor Bros. & Co. Catalogue illustrating the top hats available from their inventory.

Company, and hundreds of independent trappers traded with native populations for fur or set their own traps. The result of over two hundred years of trapping and exporting thousands of beaver skins was the near extinction of the beaver by the 1830s. What beaver fur remained became rare and extremely costly:

As the number of beavers caught annually in America has greatly declined, the price of a beaver-fur hat of late years increased; and this circumstance has led to the production of a kind of hat which presents some resemblance to beaver, and yet, may be produced at a low rate. This is the *silk* hat, the manufac-

28   TAYLOR BROS. & CO., CHICAGO, PRICE LIST.

PEARL *AND* NUTRIA

CASSIMERE

PLUG ✦ HATS

Quantity.	Price.

......Dozen No. 134, Men's Pearl Colored Plug Hats, band to
match, good ones.............................. ....$24.00

......Dozen No. 135, Men's Nutria Plug Hats, band to match.... 24.00

Every Good Prompt-paying Merchant can make money on our goods because it costs us so little to sell them, and placing an order in our hands through our Catalogue and Price List puts us under obligations to give you a better bargain than we would be expected to do if we had you in person and could argue with you *pro* and *con* as to the merits of our goods. Our goods are criticised by every competitor; we are not present upon the arrival of goods to argue the good points, and hence we are business men enough to know we must make the prices and quality speak for themselves.

Figure 39. Page from the 1889 Taylor Bros. & Co. Catalogue illustrating the top hats available from their inventory.

ture of which has gone through several stages of improvement, by which even an humble "gossamer" now presents a neat and glossy exterior.

. . . Beaver hatters look down with some little scorn on the operations of silk hatting; and certainly, so far as regards manipulative skill acquired by long practice, the former branch of handicraft is by far the most remarkable; but still the silk hat appeals with such moderation to the purse of the purchaser, that we cannot afford to lose sight of him.—"A Day at a Hat-Factory," *The Penny Magazine*, January 1841.

The beaver was saved from total extirpation along the Missouri only because the demand for pelts in the European market was drastically curtailed after 1833. The market price fell so low in the late 1830s that it was no longer profitable to trap beaver, and within a decade their numbers were replenished by natural increases.

—David J. Wishart, *The Fur Trade of the American West 1807–1840*

This reduction in demand was caused by the introduction of the silk top hat and the availability of silk from China to make them. The whims of fashion supported the change.

To make a felt hat, a felt cone, approximately nine to ten inches long after shrinking, is pulled down over a multi-pieced wooden block carved in the shape of a top hat (Figure 41). To create the brim, a string is pulled down the side of the crown and tied off where the brim starts. From that point, the wide end of the cone is gently and evenly pulled out and over the brim block; in this way an entire hat is stretched from a single cone of felt.

When fur became scarce, an alternative appeared on the scene—silk plush. Legend has it that a Mr. M. Bota, an avid traveler, went to China early in the 1800s wearing his European fur felt top hat. The hat became so worn while he was in China that Mr. Bota asked a Chinese hat maker to make him a new hat, as similar to the old one as possible. What he received was made of something soft and glossy. Upon returning to England, he startled people with his shiny top hat. But soon, as with many startling things, it became the rage; silk plush provided a much-needed substitute for the now diminishing supply of beaver fur. The majority of top hats manufactured after 1840 were made from this woven silk fabric, although, for those who could afford them, gray, brown, and dark green fur felt hats continued to be produced and appear in collections from that period.

Because fur can be dyed or bleached to virtually any hue, it allows for great variety in the coloring of top hats. Gentlemen appear to be wearing only black in the black and white illustrations of sartorial journals, but in the colored plates in *Vanity Fair,* and in descriptions in catalogues and advertisements, white, gray, dark green, and shades of brown from tan to dark maroon are shown. Silk plush,

Figure 40. A beaver, bearer of the finest felting fur, and source of the highest-quality hats. Roswell Art Museum.

Figure 41. Multiple-piece wooden top hat block and hat sizer, measuring stick, and brim iron. Stockport Heritage Museum.

however, was manufactured only in black, cream, or white. The cream-colored, long-fibered silk plush top hat was an elegant adornment (Figure 42).

Figure 42. Musician wearing a white fur felt top hat. Author's collection.

When silk plush replaced fur felt, the hats were still called "beavers" after their predecessors, because a beaver fur felt hat was the most expensive and stylish. Even today, this nomenclature leads to incorrect identification of the silk plush top hat. To determine the difference, examine the surface sheen and look for stitching between the crown top and sides or the crown bottom and brim, as well as any visible cloth texture. If the surface is one consistent texture with no stitching, it is fur or wool felt (Figure 43). If stitch marks are visible and the surface is glossy, it is silk plush.

Figure 43. Fur felt hat. Stockport Heritage Museum.

The opera hat is also covered in silk, either a plain weave or a heavier faille. According to the 1942 edition of *How Hats are Made,*

> The silk covering of the opera hat is one of its most important parts. To the eye, the silk is the hat. By the fineness of its appearance, it stimulates the "desire to buy" in the prospect, and by the strength and resiliency of its weave it must withstand endless folding of the crown.
>
> Better opera hats have a silk cloth woven of the finest grades of filature silk over a filler of the best Egyptian mercerized cotton. Cotton is used for the filler because pure silk, for this purpose, would crack.

Other materials could be shaped into a top hat, and straw was a favorite. Straws tended to duplicate the styles of the fashionable fur hats. Daniel Webster was pictured in a daguerreotype in 1848 wearing a tall straw with the wider brim that was fashionable around the late 1840s (Figure 44). As they had with the silk plush hat, coachmen adopted the straw version for summer wear. Religious groups, such as the Shakers, also duplicated their winter fur felt styles in their summer straws (Figures 45–47). Variety came not only from the hat size, but from the different plait patterns that were hand-braided and then sewn together over a wooden block of the desired size and shape.

Figure 44. Daniel Webster, 1852, wearing a straw top hat. Plate daguerreotype courtesy George Eastman House.

*Figure 45. Straw high-crown hat, similar to one worn by
Daniel Webster. Crown 5 3/4, brim 2 3/4.
Ohio Historical Society.*

*Figure 46. Fur felt, medium-crown hat, brought to Ohio in 1815 or
1818; labeled Joseph & John Galigher Brothers, hats and caps.
Ohio Historical Society.*

*Figure 47. Shaker straw hat, "Daniel Bowler." Crown 5, brim 4 1/8.
Ohio Historical Society*

Figure 48. Straw boater, crown $3^{1}/_{2}$, brim $2^{3}/_{8}$.
Author's collection.

The summer boater, so popular from 1900 onward, is a low-crowned relative of the taller top hat. It, too, can be found in dozens of brim widths and plaiting patterns (Figure 48).

Hat boxes were needed for storage and transport. Much care went into their design, resulting in a variety of styles that have today also become collectors' items. The earliest eighteenth-century boxes were made of cardboard covered in solid or wallpaper-printed paper, often replicating

Figure 49. Plain papered top-hat box, formed in the hat's shape.
Author's collection.

*Figure 50. Wallpaper-covered cardboard top-hat box
shaped like the hat. Author's collection.*

Figure 51. Leather hat box. Author's collection.

the shape of the hat (Figures 49–50). Later nineteenth-
and twentieth-century boxes were constructed of leather
and tin (Figures 51 & 53). The inside of the leather case
was padded with a red silk lining and had straps to hold
the top hat in place. A rectangular velvet pad was included
to smooth the silk plush, always in the direction of the
nap.

Figure 52. Creator of Resistol hats, Harry Rolnick, and his wife, Rose, in a holiday portrait. Harry holds an elegant gray fur felt top hat. Collection of Ken Jewell.

Figure 53. Tin hat box that has seen much traveling.
Author's collection.

The top hat has experienced extremes. Once the signature accessory of the wealthy and powerful, it has since evolved into the Dr. Seuss red-and-white-striped hat on a cat. Top hats were included in wills and handed on to relatives or servants to wear because of their expense. Even used top hats had value; they were sold by street peddlers to men of lesser means (Figure 54). Some men wore their personal favorites far beyond their stylishness, maintaining a personal appearance that felt comfortable and suited their stature, religion, or profession. It is risky, therefore, to date hats by pictorial evidence. General conventions are more accurately established.

Whatever the occasion, men appeared to wear their toppers with pride and dignity. Try to imagine a world of formality where rules of etiquette and dress were uppermost in people's minds, and you will better understand why anyone in their right mind would not only wear a "stovepipe" on his head, but revere it!

Figure 54. Used top hats being sold by street peddler.

NOTES

1. As quoted in Madeleine Ginsburg, *The Hat* (London: Studio Editions Ltd., 1988), 86.

2. J. C. Flugel, *The Psychology of Clothes* (London: Hogarth Press, 1930), 52.

3. Colin McDowell, *Hats: Status, Style and Glamour* (New York: Rizzoli, 1992), 29.

4. Ginsburg, 45–46.

5. McDowell, 28.

6. Margaret C. Conkling, *The American Gentlemen's Guide to Politeness and Fashion* (New York: Derby & Jackson, 1858), 27–31.

7. Geoffrey C. Ward, Ric Burns, and Ken Burns, *The Civil War: An Illustrated History* (New York: Alfred A. Knopf, 1990), 361.

8. Stark & Legum Catalogue 2000 (Norfolk, VA: Stark & Legum, Inc., 2000), 16.

9. Willett and Phillis Cunnington, *The Handbook of English Costume in the 19th Century* (London: Faber, 1970), 151.

*Figure 55. Collection of top hats at the Stockport Heritage Museum.
The silk plush toppers were originally dated to the early 1800s
because of their size and shape. When evaluated by Madeleine
Ginsburg, they were found to be early 20th-century reproductions
(1908 and 1909 by Tess and Co.). The tallest, an 18-inch hat
(center back), is thought to be a sales model rather than
a style that was actually worn.*

*Figure 56. More hats from the Stockport Heritage Museum
collection.*

Figure 57. Gentleman wearing silk top hat, c. 1900.
Author's collection.

APPENDICES

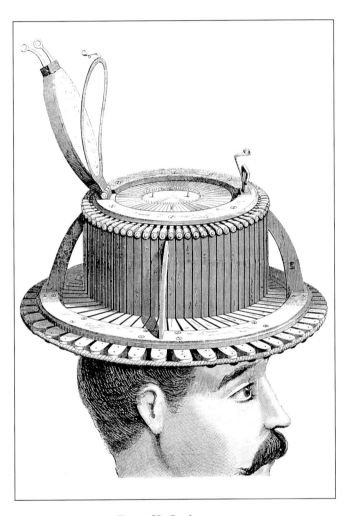

Figure 58. Conformateur.

Figure A1. A lifetime of experience goes into brim curling.

"How a Silk Hat Is Made" and *"How an Opera Hat Is Made,"* originally published in 1942, are reprinted here courtesy of Hat Life Publications.

How a Silk Hat Is Made

During the latter half of the nineteenth century, the silk hat was generally worn to business and for other informal uses. Its use today is restricted as a hat for formal and ceremonious occasions. Because of the limited volume in which such an article can be used, the silk hat industry has not in recent years attracted many young men who care to learn the difficult handcrafts required in its making. As a result, most of the personnel of the silk hat factories are past middle age, and the production of silk hats is slow and deliberate in comparison with industries which can recruit young and energetic workers and speed up their output with machinery.

The silk which is used for covering silk hats is known as hatters' plush. It is imported from France, where it is manufactured chiefly in and around the city of Lyons. It is a delicate, supple, and expensive fabric. During World War II, with French exports cut off and before silk was frozen, a satisfactory domestic product had been developed through research.

Cutting the Silk Plush

In the making of the silk hat, the first operation is the cutting of the plush. The cutter must measure and cut the material according to specifications for the sizes ordered. Great care must be taken in this operation, for just the exact amount of plush must be cut. If too much or too little material is cut, the material will form a cover which will be too large or too small to cover the hat body.

Two pieces are cut for each hat. One is cut the width of the side crown, and the other to cover the top of the crown. The plush for the top of the brim is cut later, after the crown of the body has been covered.

The two pieces of plush are then sent to the cover-sewer to be made into a complete cover for the crown. It is a delicate piece of work, and must be done entirely by hand. The stitching is done on the underside of the material and connects the top of the crown to the sides, and the sewing must be done so cleverly that the join does not form a ridge on the hat when it is completed.

Figure A2. The costly silk plush must be cut to the exact size of the hat to be made, to assure a snug-fitting covering.

The ends of the side-crown covering are not yet joined, however, as this must be done later when the cover has been fitted to the body, to avoid wrinkles.

While the cover-sewer is sewing both pieces of plush together to fit the crown, the body-maker is preparing the body to which the cover is later to be attached.

Making the Body

The rigidity and lightness of the hat are provided by a body of muslin stiffened with shellac. The making of this body is an art in itself. Several thicknesses of the muslin are used to assure the proper strength and resilience. Each thickness is a particular grade of muslin for a particular purpose—a coarse grade to give backing, a fine grade for the smooth finish, etc.

The muslin, which arrives in the factory in bolts, is cut into pieces so that these may be shellacked. Even the

Figure A3. Several layers of shellacked muslin make the crown.

Figure A4. Hot iron joins brim to crown.

order in which the pieces of muslin are shellacked is significant. For the brim, which must be absolutely rigid, the required number of layers of muslin, ranging from a very heavy grade to one that is light, are cut to fit a big wooden frame on which the layers are stretched taut, one on top of the other. The frame is then immersed in the shellac. This produces one solid layer as hard as a board. For the crown, where a more elastic "give" is desirable, each layer is shellacked separately, and all are joined later in the making of the hat.

After the muslin to be used for the brim has been completely soaked in the shellac, the frame is removed and allowed to hang for at least two days so that it will dry sufficiently.

Fashioning the Crown

The crown of the body is handled in a different manner. The muslin used on the crown is immersed in a shellac bath in individual pieces. Three grades of muslin are used for the tip of the crown, and two grades for the sides, each dipped in the shellac separately.

After it is hung up to dry for two days, the pieces go to the body-maker.

The crown of the body is made first. A piece of shellacked muslin, of a rough and heavy grade, is wound around a block. This will be the sides of the crown when the body is finished.

The block is ingenious, by the way, for it has to fit inside a hat which is curved or "belled," and still be removable after the hat is finished. This is done by using a block made of five pieces, expanded by a piece in the center. When this is removed the block collapses and drops out of the hat.

The ends of the muslin are joined with the application of heat from an iron. The heat softens the shellac and both ends of the piece on the block remain joined when the iron is removed.

Then a piece is cut to fit the top of the crown and enough allowance is made in cutting this piece so that part of it overlaps on the sides of the crown. This is joined with the hot iron to the piece already on the block. Next, a smooth, light piece of muslin is wound around the sides of the block, covering the piece already there and over-lapping the piece placed on the tip of the crown. Then, two other pieces are cut to fit the tip of the crown, *with no overlapping.* One grade, not as rough and heavy as the first piece on the tip, is used, and over this the lightest and smoothest of all, is placed. This completes the crown of the body.

Joining Crown and Brim

Then, the crown must be joined to the brim. An oval is cut in the center of the square piece of shellacked muslin that has been prepared for the brim, so that it will fit the block on which the crown was made. About three-quarters of an inch is left overlapping on the inside of the brim so that it may be joined to the sides of the crown. A little heat is applied to the inside of the brim and it is then forced over the crown already on the block. After the overlap has been joined to the crown with the hot iron, the body-maker pares it down and covers it with a thin strip of muslin, so that no ridge appears anywhere on the body.

After the outer edge of the brim has been cut to size, the body is brushed with shellac and allowed to dry for twenty-four hours.

Covering the Body

The first operation in the covering process is the placing of a strip of Merino cloth (imported from England) on the under part of the brim. It is made to adhere by ironing, which softens the shellac in the body and joins the mate-rial to the body. Then the upper part of the brim is covered in a similar manner with hatters' plush.

Then the silk hatters' plush is placed over the crown of the body so that it will cover the tip and sides. This operation must be handled carefully so that the join is not discernible. The top of the cover is then made to adhere to the crown top of the body, by the application of heat.

Then the finisher measures exactly where the join on the side-crown should be made so that both ends of the plush covering the sides will meet evenly. When this is ascertained, the nap of the plush on one end is brushed back with a fine wire brush. Then, after the end has been cut so that it meets the other end evenly, and the entire "cover" has been joined to the crown of the body, *the nap on the end of the plush which has been cut is brushed back to its natural position.* This accounts for the invisibility of the seam on the crown of a silk hat.

The partially finished hat is then given to the curler, who applies some heat to the edge of the brim. This softens the edge, and a shackle (i. e., a heated iron with a curved groove) is used to curl it. After this, wooden shackles are used on the brim while it is still flexible and the edge of the brim is given the desired curl.

There still remain slight ridges in the plush of the crown left by the edges of the sectional crown block already referred to. These must be removed by the *poutancer.* In this operation the poutancer uses what is known as a "stick"—an elliptical piece of wood covered with felt. The hat is placed on the "stick" and finishing touches are made with a tolliker, a curved iron. This is a delicate job, as the "stick" does not fit the inside of the crown as the block does. The operation gives the plush a finished appearance.

The brim and crown have now been covered. The hat goes to the foreman of the shop, and the hat is either passed on to be completed, or it is rejected and must go back to the poutancer to be given additional finish.

When the hat is passed it goes to the trimmer, who binds the edge of the brim with grosgrain ribbon. Then the hat is lined and the sweat leather whipped in by hand.

Then the band is put on. This is usually a piece of black broadcloth which has been cut and sewed to the proper width and is put on by hand.

Finally, a hot cloth is passed over the plush on the brim and crown, giving it the finishing touch or "slacking," after which the hat is ready to be packed for shipment.

*Figure A5. The fitted silk plush covering is slipped over the
shellacked body, then made to adhere by
the application of a hot iron.*

Figure A6. Making the tip—(1) A tip made of 3 layers of shellacked muslin which is as "stiff as a board." Note shallow side. (2) A flexible strip of single-layer, shellacked muslin has been ironed to the side of the tip. (3) Workman turns the flexible strip over the top ring of the Gibus spring and irons it to the underside of the tip. That is a special iron, not a knife, which the man is using. Heat softens shellac and causes adherence. (4) The tip is now securely fastened to the spring and is ready to be covered with dull, grosgrain silk.

Figure A7. Covering the brim—(1) The uncovered brim of shellacked muslin. Inner edge is turned up to be fitted inside the bottom ring of Gibus spring later. (2) The underside of the brim is covered first. (3) Ironing on the upper brim. Silk for upper brim has center cut out first. Under brim was ironed on first, cut out later. Silk adheres to heat-softened shellac. (4) Both under brim and upper brim have been covered. All that remains is trimming of edges, and curling of the brim, after which brim is sent, with the tip, to the sewing room.

How an Opera Hat Is Made

Many products go into the making of an opera hat—the collapsible spring, muslin, shellac, and silk—but chief among all the "makings" is the skill of the hatmakers who produce these hats entirely by hand. In this age in which mechanical production is everywhere exalted, the opera hat is one of the outstanding remaining examples of hand craftsmanship.

The Gibus Spring

The "works" of the opera hat is its spring. Of all the mechanical contrivances for hats which have been invented, this spring is the only one which has survived. It is the brainchild of Antoine Gibus, a Paris hatter, who patented his idea in 1837.

At that time, theatre-going and the high silk hat were both tremendously popular, and the overcrowding in checkrooms was acute. The Gibus hat eliminated the congestion as if by magic, and immediately took the fancy of gentlemen the world over, who then wore top hats both for business and recreation, and who had long been impatient with the inconvenience of the rigid, high silk hat.

Except for the covering, the present-day opera hat is practically unchanged from the first ones ever produced. The covering for the first hats was the napped silk plush used for high silk hats, but upon finding that this material cracked, Mr. Gibus, himself, switched to dull grosgrain silk, such as is used today.

Preparing Stock

The first steps in the manufacture of an opera hat are grouped under the head of "preparing stock." This stock

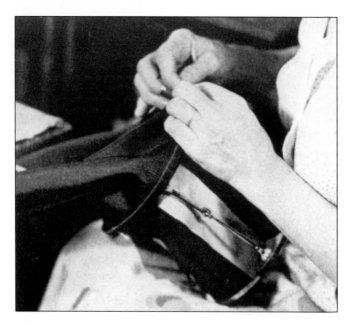

Figure A8. There are a multitude of sewing operations in opera hat making. The lining and the side crown are cut to fit and sewed to shape before they are attached to the hat. In the photo, the lining has already been sewed to the tip, and the sewer is beginning to sew the side crown to the tip. When finished, it will be pulled down, and sewed around the bottom ring of the spring. Meanwhile, another sewer is machine-hemming a strip of grosgrain ribbon to the upper brim, near the edge. This will later be turned over the edge, and hand-hemmed to the under brim to finish the edge.

Figure A9. After covering the side crown, the crown and brim are sewed together as shown in photo. The band, sewed on next, covers all stitches. Note the four cloth strips in the crown of the hat. One end of each strip has already been sewed to the tip of the lining. Other end is sewed to the headband. Each strip is then adjacent to a spring, and protects the lining when springs collapse. Next a comfort-insert is sewed around headband. Lining is then sewed to headband, completing inside. Grosgrain ribbon is turned around brim edge and sewing is finished.

is the material over which the grosgrain silk is laid. It is fine muslin, stiffened by impregnation with orange shellac.

The quality of this shellac is one of the important factors determining the strength of the finished hat. Better-quality shellac is imported from India, and is very carefully prepared.

There are two kinds of stock, (1) tip stock, for the top (or "tip") of the crown, and (2) brim stock.

The tip is made of 3-ply stock—three layers of muslin, impregnated and pressed together to form one sheet. The muslin is cut in strips about three feet by four feet. The strips are dipped in the shellac vat, wrung out, and stretched one atop another on a wooden frame. The frame is studded with nails which pierce the muslin and hold it like an ordinary curtain stretcher holds a curtain. The pieces are rubbed and pressed against one another until they adhere.

For brim stock, 4-ply, and sometimes 5-ply, muslin is used to provide the required extra stiffness.

The muslin is allowed to dry thoroughly at room temperature, with the drying time varying from two days to a week, depending upon the weather. The stock, when dry, is stiff—just as stiff as the brim and tip of the finished hat.

It is then removed from the frame, and cut into rectangles of approximately brim size and tip size. About twelve brims are cut from each sheet, and about thirty-six tips.

Making the Tip and the Brim

The tip, like most other parts of the opera hat, is carefully made to head size. A tip block of correct size is laid on one of the rectangles of tip stock, and its outline is marked. The cutter adds one-quarter inch to the guide mark, which in the next operation, ironing on the tip block, is turned down to form a shallow side.

A strip of 1-ply stock one-half inch wide is ironed to the side of the tip. The iron softens the shellac, so that the strip (which hatmakers call the "robbin") adheres readily. The top ring of the Gibus spring is now set in the tip, and the robbin turned over the ring and ironed to the underside of the tip. For this operation, the hatter has a special iron which closely resembles a linoleum knife, and with which he can reach with ease between the springs.

The tip is next "finished"—covered with dull, grosgrain silk. The tip finisher brushes a thin coating of special tip shellac on the tip, and then, with his hands and brush, carefully presses on a rectangle of silk roughly cut to size. The silk is turned around the top ring of the spring and ironed to the robbin so that it covers the side as well as the top of the tip. Ends are trimmed.

A Note on the Silk

The silk covering of the opera hat is one of its most important parts. To the eye, the silk is the hat. By the fineness of its appearance, it stimulates the "desire to buy" in the prospect, and by the strength and resiliency of its weave it must withstand endless folding of the crown.

Better opera hats have a silk cloth woven of the finest grades of filature silk over a filler of the best Egyptian mercerized cotton. Cotton is used for the filler because pure silk, for this purpose, would crack.

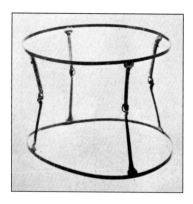

Figure A10. The Gibus spring is the "works" of the opera hat. It was invented 105 years ago by Antoine Gibus, Paris hatmaker. Hence another name for the opera hat is the "Gibus Hat." This hat is the only mechanical hat, of the scores which have been patented, which has been a success. It solved a serious hat-checking problem in France at a time when high-hat wearing and opera-going were at their heights. From France, the hat's popularity spread around the world, for gentlemen of many countries then wore top hats for both pleasure and business. Mr. Gibus' first hats were covered with napped silk plush, but he himself changed the covering to dull grosgrain silk when he found that the plush cracked. Thus the opera hat today is almost unchanged from those of a century ago.

Cutting the Brim

The rectangle of brim stock is first marked with the headsize block, and the center cut out. The inner edge of the brim is to be turned up just as the outer edge of the tip was turned down, so the cutter cuts one-quarter inch inside the block mark. Brim is ironed on a special block which drops the front and the back slightly; and the inner edge is turned up.

The outer edge of the brim is marked with a rounding jack that has been set to allow the extra width which will be taken up by the brim curl later. Thus marked, the brim is cut to shape with rounding shears.

Brim is now ready to be finished. Two rectangles of grosgrain silk, cut roughly to size, are at hand.

Unlike the method of covering the tip through the adhesive properties of a special tip shellac, the grosgrain is made to adhere to the brim merely by ironing.

The brim then goes to the curler who gives the brim its curl and flare at the sides. The brim and the spring are now sent to the sewing room.

Sewing the Hat

The first step in sewing is the only machine operation in the entire manufacture of the hat. This is the hemming of one edge of a strip of grosgrain ribbon all around the upper brim, near the edge. This strip is later turned over the edge and hemmed by hand to the under brim, thus "finishing" the edge.

The lining of the opera hat, and the covering for the side crown are cut to size and sewed to the shape before the operator begins to attach them to the hat.

The operator first sews the tip of the lining to the top ring of the spring. She then turns to the outside of the hat, and sews the side crown to the tip. Thus fastened at the top, the side crown is pulled downward, and its lower edge stitched around the bottom ring of the spring.

The crown is set on the brim, fitting just around that turned-up inner edge. Operator stitches them together. The band is next sewed to the hat. It covers the stitches which have fastened the brim to the crown.

When the lining was prepared, there was sewed on the outside at the tip four strips of protective cloth to lie next to the four springs of the hat. *They protect the lining from the springs which collapse inward, and might damage the lining.* These strips are now pulled taut and the lower ends sewed onto the headband. Another piece of material, very soft, is then sewed all around the headband. Its purpose is to soften the feel of the hat on the head.

With these unseen construction steps concluded, the operator sews the lower edge of the lining to the headband of the hat. All that remains is turning the grosgrain ribbon along the brim edge and hemming it to the under brim.

The hat is sent back to the forming shop where the brim is given a final curl, and set, and the entire hat is inspected.

Gentleman wearing his hat at a jaunty angle. Author's collection.

Comical scene with man wearing a stovepipie top hat.
Author's collection.

Unknown gentleman wearing a silk top hat, c. 1860.
Author's collection.

Bibliography

"Atherstone Hatters, The," Atherstone, Warwickshire: Wilson & Stafford Limited, 1998.

Bath Museum of Costume. Hat Collection, 1996, 1997.

Bucks County Historical Society, Mercer Museum. Hat Collection, 1995.

Chicago Historical Society. Hat Collection, 1995.

Christy & Co. Catalogues 1842, 1899, 1911 and 1916. Stockport: The Christy Hat Company, 1842, 1899, 1911, and 1916.

Cincinnati Art Museum. Hat Collection. Cincinnati, Ohio, 1994, 1999.

Conkling, Margaret C. *The American Gentlemen's Guide to Politeness and Fashion.* New York: Derby and Jackson, 1858.

Cunnington, Willett and Phillis. *The Handbook of English Costume in the 19th Century.* London: Faber, 1970.

"Day at a Hat-Factory, A." *The Penny Magazine,* January 1841.

Dony, J. G. *A History of the Straw Hat Industry.* Luton, England: Luton Museum and Art Gallery, 1942.

Druesedow, Jean L., editor. *Men's Fashion Illustrations from the Turn of the Century.* New York: Dover Publications, 1990.

Flugel, J. C. *The Psychology of Clothes.* London: Hogarth Press, 1930.

Freeman, Charles. *Luton and the Hat Industry.* Luton: The Borough of Luton Museum and Art Gallery, 1953.

Ginsburg, Madeleine. *The Hat.* London: Studio Editions, 1990.

How Hats Are Made. New York: Hat Life, 1942.

Hulme, Roger. Interview by author. Stockport, England, 19 July 1994.

Indianapolis Children's Museum. Hat Collection, 1995.

Kent State University Museum. Hat Collection, 1994.

McDowell, Colin. *Hats: Status, Style and Glamour.* New York: Rizzoli, 1992.

Metropolitan Museum of Art Costume Institute. Hat Collection, 1995.

Musée du Chapeau. Hat Collection. Chazelles-sur-Lyon, France, 1998.

Ohio Historical Society. Hat Collection. Columbus, Ohio, 1994.

Philadelphia History Museum: The Atwater Kent. Hat Collection, 1998.

Sartor, The, or British Journal of Cutting, Clothing, and Fashion. London, England (Vol. 1–3, 2 November 1870–20 March 1873).

Sartorial Art Journal. New York (1891–1910).

Stark & Legum Catalogue 2000. Norfolk, VA: Stark & Legum, Inc., 2000.

Stockport Heritage Museum. Hat Collection. Stockport, England, 1995, 1997.

Victoria and Albert Museum. Hat Collection. London, England, 1998.

Ward, Geoffrey C., Ric Burns, and Ken Burns, *The Civil War: An Illustrated History.* New York: Alfred A. Knopf, 1990.

Western Reserve Historical Society. Hat Collection. Cleveland, Ohio, 1995.

Wishart, David J. *The Fur Trade of the American West, 1807–1840.* Lincoln, NB: University of Nebraska Press, 1992.

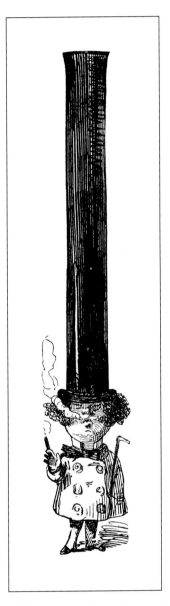

The top hat was sometimes taken to extremes.

About the Author

Debbie Henderson is currently the costume designer for the Wittenberg University Theatre Department and the costume and scenic designer for Clark State College, both in Springfield, Ohio. In her work, Dr. Henderson researches clothing worn in other centuries and other countries while attempting to discover the attitudes clothing conveys and inspires. This interest prompted her interdisciplinary doctoral work on the history and manufacture of the man's hat, undertaken through the Union Institute in Cincinnati, Ohio. Her research resulted in the creation of an exhibit about the man's hat that contains over a hundred hats and related visual materials, and which has been shown at museums around the country. She is also a designer of residential and commercial spaces. Dr. Henderson is the author of *Cowboys & Hatters: Bond Street, Sagebrush, & the Silver Screen* (Wild Goose Press, 1996) and of numerous journal articles.